ManagerOS™: Upgrade Your Career

Reboot Your Management Operating System (OS). Accelerate Your Success.

Peter M. Badger

ISBN: 979-8-9993152-0-5

Table of Contents

Preface

Management and leadership emerge not from theory but from experience—often challenging, sometimes humbling, and ultimately rewarding. This book draws on more than three decades of navigating global financial institutions, a tech startup, and various corporate transformations across four continents.

I'm deeply grateful to the extraordinary teams I've had the privilege to manage and lead, from my early days in London, New York, Tokyo, Hong Kong, and San Francisco. From Morgan Stanley through to Framehawk. My early mentors—Kumud Kalia, Dick Taggart, and Derek Stein—taught me patience, wisdom, and their tools of the trade, especially the power of listening (which I'm still practicing daily!). Later in my career, advisors and colleagues—Charlie Oppenheimer, Stephen Vilke, Iain Greer, Simon Hayes, Matt Wren—helped me round out additional skills. Meanwhile, my closest family members endured the demands of global management and constant house moves, while a litany of people, too many to mention, helped me transform all of these insights into the book you now hold.

To my book writing friends—Guillaume Devred-Smith, Olivier Roland, Chris Morgan—who instilled the belief in me that I could follow in their footsteps, and both write and publish a book.

These pages contain lessons about building high-performing teams while nurturing individual growth. My hope is that these experiences—both successes and the occasional instructive failure—will guide your management and leadership journey.

To my wife Keke, thank you for your sacrifice, patience, and unwavering support through countless moves and challenges these last few years. To my brother Andrew, your advice and steadfast encouragement made this book possible.

And to our children Mike, Luke, Ella, and Lucy, I hope these lessons make your own paths in managing and leading yourselves and others smoother than mine was.

This book is ultimately dedicated to those who understand that management is not about authority, but about service through leadership—to your team, your organization, and a purpose greater than yourself.

- Peter M. Badger

Prologue: Management versus Leadership

"You'll grow with the job."

Management and leadership are related but distinct concepts with important differences:

Management typically focuses on:

- Executing processes and systems
- Controlling resources and coordinating activities
- Planning, organizing, staffing, and monitoring
- Maintaining stability and efficiency
- Solving problems within established frameworks
- Position-based authority

Leadership typically focuses on:

- Creating vision and inspiring change
- Influencing and motivating people
- Building relationships and developing talent
- Challenging the status quo and driving innovation
- Creating new paths and possibilities
- Personal influence that extends beyond formal authority

While these concepts overlap considerably, and good managers are often good leaders (and vice versa), they aren't perfectly interchangeable. Using them interchangeably can sometimes blur important distinctions:

- You can be in a management position without demonstrating strong leadership
- You can be a leader without having a formal management title
- Organizations need both effective management and inspirational leadership

For someone starting out in management, focusing on foundational management skills first is generally the wisest approach. Strong technical management skills create credibility and stability. Learn to plan effectively, allocate resources, establish clear processes, and monitor results. These fundamentals form the platform from which leadership can emerge.

While both management and leadership are ultimately essential, new managers who try to lead transformative change before mastering day-to-day operations often struggle. Your team needs to trust that you can handle the basics before they'll follow you into uncharted territory. Consider developing in phases: first master operational management (scheduling, resource allocation, performance monitoring), then add people management skills (delegation, feedback, development, difficult conversations), and finally incorporate leadership elements (vision-setting, innovation, inspirational motivation).

Different contexts demand different emphasis. A team in crisis needs strong management first. A high-performing, stable team might benefit more from leadership that stretches them toward new possibilities. Look for small ways to demonstrate leadership while building management skills. This might include championing a process improvement, mentoring a team member, or proposing a thoughtful innovation to senior leadership.

As someone who managed teams across global organizations, I learned that respect is earned first through competent management before you can effectively inspire as a leader. The most successful new managers build a strong technical foundation while gradually expanding their leadership capabilities. The journey from manager to leader is rarely linear, but rather an organic evolution where proven competence creates the trust needed for influential leadership.

Being good at both management and leadership is the ultimate goal as your career progresses. This book is about management fundamentals with some leadership sprinkled in, especially when it comes to managing teams.

Introduction

I pride myself on being approachable.

When I was promoted to my first management position at 26 years old, I vividly recall the mix of pride and panic I felt. I had built my career on technical expertise and hard work, and I assumed those same skills would make me a great manager. In fact, I thought being a boss simply meant delegating most of the work I used to do. Within a few months, reality smacked me in the face. My team was missing deadlines, I was working longer hours than ever, and one of my best employees quit unexpectedly. I remember riding the NYC subway after work one evening, wondering, "What am I doing wrong?" The hard truth hit me: the very skills that got me promoted weren't enough to succeed in this new role. I realized I needed to fundamentally upgrade my own operating system as a professional – my mindset, skills, and approach – if I wanted to thrive as a manager.

That epiphany was the seed for what I've come to call **ManagerOS**, an operating system for managers. Just like a computer's OS, a manager's operating system needs periodic upgrades to handle new challenges and increased complexity. Over my 35-year corporate career, I went through many "version updates" of my **ManagerOS**. With each new level of responsibility – from managing myself on day one, to managing a small team, then entire departments, and eventually leading the whole company – I had to learn new ways of managing and then leading. Every promotion was like installing a major software update. Some updates went smoothly; others crashed and forced me to reboot my approach entirely. I wrote this book to share those lessons and help you upgrade your own **ManagerOS** more smoothly, without the hard reboots I had to endure.

This journey starts with the most fundamental component: **self-management**. The first person you must effectively manage is yourself. I learned (often the hard way) that if I couldn't manage my own time, energy, and growth, I had little hope of managing others. In my early career, I struggled with long hours and burnout until a mentor bluntly told me, "You're no good to your team if you're running on empty." I began to appreciate classic wisdom like Peter Drucker's advice to "know thyself" – understand your strengths, weaknesses, and how you work best. I also discovered the power of habits and personal organization, realizing that my productivity systems and the example I set would set the tone for my entire team. Self-management became the bedrock of my effectiveness before I could manage others.

Next, I had to learn the art of **managing up**. Early in my journey, I had a boss who was extremely hands-off – to the point of being absent. I was tasked with running an important project, but I needed guidance and buy-in from senior stakeholders. At first, I thought positional authority was my only tool (after all, I was the manager on paper). I soon learned that real influence doesn't come from a title. It comes from trust, communication, and understanding what others need. Managing up taught me how to build a strong relationship with my own bosses and other executives – to "manage my boss" in a positive way. Rather than seeing it as manipulation or flattery, I discovered that managing up means being the most effective employee you can be, creating value for your boss and your company. In practice, that meant keeping my superiors informed (no surprises), framing issues in terms of their priorities, and eventually learning to diplomatically lead my bosses when they were too busy or heading in the wrong direction. These skills became crucial as I climbed the ladder, because no matter how senior you get, there's always someone above you or key stakeholders you don't directly control. Management and leadership, I found, is a 360-degree exercise.

Of course, managing up is only part of the equation – I also had to learn to **manage down**, to become the boss that people actually want to work for. This was perhaps the hardest lesson, because it required confronting some truths about myself. I'll never forget one of my earliest one-on-one meetings with a team member named "Keith." I launched right into a status update, asking if he'd met the week's targets. He responded with frustration that he wasn't getting any guidance or feedback from me, only pressure. That stung, but he was right. In my push for results, I had neglected the fundamentals of people management – clear communication, encouragement, and support.

Over time, I devoured research on what makes a great manager and reflected on the best (and worst) bosses I'd had. I learned that employees leave managers, not companies, as the old saying goes. In fact, a Gallup poll found 75% of workers who quit their jobs do so at least in part because of issues with their boss. I was determined not to be that boss. Instead, I aimed to be a coach, advisor, and a mentor, not just a taskmaster. I began having regular one-on-ones focused on my team members' growth, practicing "radical candor" (being honest while showing I care), and making sure people felt recognized for their contributions. The transformation was remarkable – not just in morale, but in performance. When people feel supported and trust their manager, they give their best. I saw it firsthand, and research backs it up (for example, Google's extensive study "Project Oxygen" confirmed that effective managers who coach, communicate, and care drive better team outcomes). Becoming the boss people want to work for isn't about being easy or nice all the time – it's about balancing empathy with accountability. In Chapter 3, I'll share the frameworks and principles that can help you strike that balance, from establishing trust to delivering feedback in a way that motivates.

As my scope grew, I faced a new challenge: **managing teams and leading through others**. It's one thing to manage individuals; it's another to cultivate an entire team's culture and performance. I remember when I was first put in charge of a cross-functional team of 20+ people spread across three countries. I couldn't possibly be in every meeting or know every detail – I had to build a self-sufficient team and empower others to lead themselves. In other words, I had to evolve from a manager into what I now call a multiplier. This concept, inspired by Liz Wiseman's book, *Multipliers: How the Best Leaders Make Everyone Smarter (Harper Business, 2017)*, means using your leadership to amplify the capability of your team, rather than stifling it.

I learned to spot the difference: Was I acting as a Multiplier, bringing out people's best and getting "more brainpower" from the group, or was I unintentionally acting as a Diminisher, bottlenecking decisions and hoarding control? Through some trial and error, I discovered that the best teams excel when the manager focuses on setting vision, enabling collaboration, and then getting out of the way. It became my job to clear obstacles, secure resources, and let my people shine – not to have my hands in every pie. I also learned the importance of psychological safety on teams – a term coined by Harvard's Amy Edmondson, and later reinforced by Google's "Project Aristotle" research, which found that teams with a high degree of trust and psychological safety outperform others. In practice, that meant encouraging healthy debate, admitting my own mistakes, and ensuring everyone's voice was heard. Chapter 4 will delve into how you sometimes have to change your **ManagerOS** style to meet the ability and maturity of your team so you can cultivate a team environment where individuals synergize into something greater – where you produce multiplicative results and even develop the next generation of leaders.

Then came perhaps my biggest management challenge yet: navigating the transition to **managing remote employees**. As our workforce became increasingly distributed, I had to develop entirely new skills for managing people I rarely saw in person. I faced unique obstacles: How do you build trust without face-to-face interaction? How do you foster engagement from afar? How do you detect wellbeing issues despite physical distance? I discovered that remote management requires intentional communication rhythms that prevent isolation without causing meeting fatigue. It demands new approaches to maintaining productivity while honoring work-life boundaries that blur when home becomes the office. Most challengingly, it requires creating team cohesion when members work across different time zones and cultures. Through experimentation and drawing on emerging research, I developed strategies that not only overcame these challenges but actually leveraged the unique advantages of distributed work. Chapter 5 will explore these approaches in depth, helping you adapt your management style for our increasingly digital workplace.

Throughout this book, I will share these experiences and the lessons they taught me, always in the context of practical frameworks you can apply. You'll see references to management literature and research, not because theory is more important than practice, but because I found validation and guidance in those frameworks during my journey. For example, only after I struggled with burnout did I appreciate Stephen Covey's matrix of urgent vs. important tasks, which taught me to prioritize what truly matters rather than just react to fires. Only after fumbling with a difficult boss did I discover the art of influence without authority, reminiscent of the Cohen-Bradford model of exchanging "organizational currencies" to get buy-in. I want to equip you not just with my anecdotes, but also with proven models from the world of business and psychology that can guide you through your own challenges.

The structure of the book mirrors the layers of managerial and leadership skills I had to build over 35 years and continue to evolve:

Self-Management – Because every great manager I've met agrees on one thing: you can't manage others if you don't deepen your own self-awareness and show others how to manage emotions.

Managing Up – Which is about leading when you're not in charge (a reality for managers at every level).

Managing Individuals – Focuses on the direct management of individuals – essentially, how to be the kind of boss that brings out the best in people.

Managing Teams – Elevates the discussion to managing groups and scaling your impact, the step from being a good manager to a great leader or "multiplier."

Managing Remote Employees – Addresses the unique *challenges and opportunities* of managing distributed teams across time zones and cultures in our increasingly digital workplace.

Along the way, you'll find personal stories, key concepts explained, frameworks to illuminate why certain approaches work, and plenty of practical examples. Each chapter ends with a summary of actionable takeaways – think of these as upgrade patches for your own **ManagerOS**.

My goal is to make this journey engaging and useful. The tone you'll find here is part seasoned corporate coach, part fellow traveler who's still able to laugh at his own mistakes. Management is a serious responsibility, but it doesn't mean we can't smile or share a chuckle about the quirks of office life and the universal "facepalm" moments every manager endures. I want you to feel like we're sitting down for a candid conversation about what it really takes to manage – the good and the bad.

By the end of this book, I hope you'll come away with two things. First, a toolkit of ideas and techniques you can start applying on Monday morning – whether it's a new way to prioritize your tasks, a script for a tough conversation with your boss, or a method to build trust with your team. Second, a mindset shift: an understanding that becoming a better manager (and advancing your career) is an ongoing process of learning and growth. In a world that's constantly changing, the best managers are those who keep updating themselves. In fact, one study noted that 71% of employers value emotional intelligence – a trait you develop over time – more than IQ or technical skills in management roles. As Daniel Goleman put it, "The most effective managers are all alike in one crucial way: They all have a high degree of...emotional intelligence...IQ and technical skills are important, but they are entry-level requirements." In other words, to truly upgrade your career, you must continuously upgrade your managerial operating system.

So, whether you're a newly promoted manager finding your footing, or a mid-level manager looking to reach the next level, I invite you to join me in this exploration. Think of this book as a user's manual for **ManagerOS** version 2.0 (and 3.0, and beyond). The lessons ahead are drawn from decades of experience, backed by research, and tested in the real world. They helped me transform from an overwhelmed first-time manager into a confident manager who eventually led global teams and large organizations. I'm confident that, with these insights, you too can accelerate your growth and avoid some of the pitfalls that ensnared me.

I wish this book had been written when I was struggling to adapt to different management situations in the early stages of my career, or even later when I started my own company.

If you've found this book in your 20's and 30's, congratulations, you're ahead of the pack. You'll notice I reference a lot of other author's books throughout. This is to provide context and validation to the **ManagerOS** fundamentals I've learned through hard experience and put into practice myself.

It's time to begin the upgrade. Let's start with the one person you'll always manage in every job you hold – yourself.

1

Self-Management (The First Person To Manage Is You)

You Can't Manage Others If You Can't Manage Yourself

My first few months as a manager were a blur—back-to-back meetings, overflowing inbox, and late nights playing catch-up. I was constantly reacting rather than managing, exhausted rather than energized, and increasingly ineffective. I didn't have mental space for strategic thinking or meaningful team support because I hadn't learned to manage myself first. The wake-up call came when a respected colleague commented: "Peter, you constantly look frantic around your team. What's going on?" Those words landed with uncomfortable clarity.

What I discovered through trial and error is what exceptional managers understand intuitively: self-management forms the foundation for all other management skills. Without it, you're just borrowing authority from a title. With it, you become someone others genuinely trust, willingly follow, and confidently rely upon.

The Management Myth: It Doesn't Start with People

The most persistent myth about management is that it primarily involves managing others. The reality? Your first and most crucial management responsibility is yourself—your habits, energy, schedule, and responses.

Early in my career, I made the classic mistake of believing good management meant putting everyone else first. I'd dive into solving team problems without addressing my own fundamental issues with time management, emotional regulation, and mental resilience. The inevitable result was burnout. Ironically, my team felt more destabilized because I wasn't modeling the calm, clarity, and consistency they needed.

Truly effective managers operate from a stable center; the inner kernel of the **ManagerOS**. They aren't frantically racing between emergencies—instead, they move with deliberate purpose, maintain organized systems, and demonstrate emotional composure. This isn't just a nice-to-have; it's the essential baseline. Without self-management, no other levels of management can take root.

The 3 Domains of Self-Management

Self-management breaks down into three critical domains that every manager must master:

1. Time Management

You don't find time—you intentionally create it. My transformation began when I started treating my calendar as sacred territory: blocking 90-minute windows for deep work, building 30-minute buffers before important meetings, and conducting weekly CEO-style reviews of my priorities. I learned the power of saying no to "quick chats" that derailed productivity, batched email processing into specific windows, and established a proper end-of-day shutdown ritual. Gradually, my days transformed from frantic to focused.

> **🚀 Try this:** Open your calendar now and honestly assess whether it reflects your values and priorities. Are your most strategic initiatives protected with dedicated time blocks? Or is your schedule merely a collection of other people's priorities?

2. Energy Management

Management is fundamentally a high-performance endeavor. If you fail to manage your energy, you'll inevitably crash. I began treating my physical and mental well-being as critical assets: prioritizing a walk or journaling, mindful nutrition, and intentional breaks between meetings to reset. I stopped viewing rest as an indulgence and recognized it as strategic necessity. I also became deliberate about managing emotional energy: limiting unnecessarily draining interactions, preparing thoroughly for difficult conversations, and creating space for recovery.

Think of your energy like a financial account. If you're constantly withdrawing without making deposits, going broke is inevitable.

3. Focus Management

Multitasking is a destructive illusion. Every task switch exacts a cognitive penalty that compounds throughout your day. I implemented practical solutions: disabling desktop notifications, getting rid of my Apple Watch, utilizing full-screen work modes, and consolidating tasks within a single trusted system. David Allen's Getting Things Done methodology became my framework for maintaining an "external brain" that reduced mental clutter.

> 🚀 **Try this:** Adopt a daily practice of asking: "What's the one thing that, if accomplished well today, will create the most significant forward momentum?" Planning each day when you wake up in the morning and the discipline of writing that one thing in your journal or notebook will prove transformative.

Your Personal Operating System

Self-management ultimately means building your own internal operating system. This OS determines how you:

- Structure your day
- Approach decision-making
- Respond under pressure
- Establish and maintain boundaries
- Monitor progress
- Recover from setbacks

My personal OS includes daily reflective journaling, a comprehensive weekly review ritual, and absolute clarity around my top three objectives each quarter. There are many journals out there, but the one sold by **https://bestself.co/** is my go-to-system for planning and documenting my daily, weekly, quarterly goals, and tracking my daily habits. I've always believed that writing things down makes it real and manifests into concrete actions.

I also do a yearly review and reflect what went well and what I'd like to do differently the following year to ensure alignment to my long-term personal objectives.

If you don't consciously design your own system, you'll inevitably inherit someone else's—and it probably won't serve your unique needs and goals.

Framework: The Personal Dashboard

Here's a practical framework I've shared with the many people I've mentored over the years:

Personal Dashboard Template

- **Focus for the Week:** (Strategic priorities that deserve your best energy)
- **Meetings to Prepare For:** (Which conversations require deeper thought?)
- **People to Develop:** (Who needs your coaching attention this week?)
- **Energy Check:** (On a scale of 1–10, where are you and why?)
- **Boundaries to Hold:** (What specifically will you decline or defer?)
- **One Win to Celebrate:** (Acknowledging progress creates momentum)

Try this: Dedicating just 30 minutes every Monday morning to completing this dashboard can anchor your entire week in intentionality.

Note: I sometimes do this exercise on a Sunday evening if I'm stressing about the week ahead - this often improves my sleep and avoids starting Monday with a compounding sleep deficit that rolls through my week!

Use Case: The Calendar That Changed Everything

I once coached a newly promoted manager who constantly felt overwhelmed and ineffective. We conducted a thorough calendar audit and discovered that 85% of her time was consumed by meetings she neither needed to lead nor attend. Together, we systematically eliminated non-essential commitments, established protected blocks for deep work, and implemented a morning review routine. Within a month, her productivity improved—and her team noticed the difference. "You seem calmer," one team member observed. "You're more present when we talk." That's the transformative power of self-management. It's not selfish—it's the highest form of service to your team.

Key Takeaways

↳ You are the first and most important person you'll ever manage.

↳ Mastering time, energy, and focus unlocks your full potential as a manager and leader.

↳ Building a personal operating system keeps you clear, calm, and intentional.

↳ Great management begins with showing up as your best self—both for yourself and for those who depend on you.

Head over to **https://www.manageros.work/chapter1** for additional information and templates.

2

Managing Up - Leading Without Authority

Here's where we're looking for
uncomprehending nods of approval.

The Hidden Management Discipline

"Do you know what's going on with your boss?" My colleague's question caught me off guard as we waited for our next meeting to begin.

"What do you mean?"

"The reorganization. He's fighting to keep our department intact. I thought you'd be helping him build the business case."

I felt my face flush. I had no idea our department was at risk—or that my boss was in a political battle on our behalf. While I'd been heads-down managing projects and my team, I'd completely neglected to manage the relationship that could make or break our future.

That moment taught me a crucial lesson: managing isn't just about managing those who report to you. It's about managing in all directions—including upward. The most effective managers are those who can influence without authority, navigate organizational dynamics skillfully, and build strong relationships with those above them.

This essential skill—"managing up"—often marks the difference between good managers and great ones. Those who master it secure more resources for their teams, gain more support for their initiatives, and create more opportunities for growth. Those who neglect it often wonder why their projects get deprioritized and their efforts go unrecognized—regardless of how well they manage their direct reports.

Why Managing Up Matters

Management doesn't exist in isolation—it's part of an interconnected corporate ecosystem where your effectiveness depends heavily on relationships beyond your direct team. In modern corporations, managers operate within complex matrix structures, competing priorities, and resource constraints. Managing up isn't optional—it's essential for creating the conditions where your team can succeed.

Managing up isn't manipulation or flattery. It's about building productive, trust-based relationships with senior leadership so you can align priorities, gain buy-in, and make your team more effective. When you manage up effectively, you:

- Secure the support and resources your team needs
- Position yourself as a strategic partner rather than just an executor
- Build influence across organizational levels
- Navigate competing priorities and minimize unnecessary conflicts
- Shield your team from organizational turbulence

Ultimately, you distinguish yourself as someone ready for greater management responsibility while creating an environment where your team can deliver meaningful results.

The 3 Pillars of Managing Up

There are three fundamental pillars every manager needs to master when managing upward:

1. Understand Their World

Every manager above you operates with unique pressures, preferences, and priorities. Some want daily updates; others prefer weekly summaries. Some focus on vision; others on execution details. Your first task is to become a student of your manager's world.

When I reported to a data-driven CTO, he wanted metric-focused updates with specific technical performance indicators, system reliability statistics, and development velocity metrics. My next boss, a visionary COO, preferred narrative updates centered on operational improvements, cross-functional collaboration wins, and how our processes were enhancing the customer experience. Same information, completely different packaging.

 Try this: Create a "Boss User Manual" by documenting:

- How they prefer to receive information
- When they're most receptive to discussions
- Whether they prefer options or recommendations
- Which metrics and outcomes matter most to them
- What current pressures and priorities shape their thinking

Understanding isn't just about preferences—it's about empathy. What keeps your boss up at night? What success metrics are they measured against? When you understand their world and weekly flow, you can position your work to support their goals.

2. Align Priorities and Actions

The second pillar focuses on ensuring your work connects directly to what matters most to your manager and the organization. If you're solving problems that aren't on their radar, you'll struggle to get meaningful support.

When I led a program management office overseeing a complex business divestiture, I initially struggled to get executive attention. My team was focused on detailed transition plans and technical separation activities, but our COO was laser-focused on minimizing business disruption and maintaining customer confidence during the transition. Once I reframed our progress reports to highlight how our separation workstreams were protecting revenue and ensuring business continuity for key clients, I secured additional resources and the executive attention we needed.

Alignment requires regular calibration. For each of your top priorities, can you draw a direct line to your manager's key objectives? If not, you may need to:

- Refocus your efforts on higher-impact areas
- Better communicate the connection between your work and organizational goals
- Have a candid conversation about priorities

 Try this: Align your priorities with your boss' or the firm's strategic objectives to increase impact and gain more recognition.

3. Communicate Strategically

Communication isn't just about frequency—it's about strategy. Being concise, focusing on what matters to your audience, and framing information effectively are critical skills.

I learned this lesson as CEO when I sent our chairman of the board a comprehensive 10-page proposal on our new product direction, only to have him respond: "I don't have time to digest all this before the board meeting. What's the bottom line?" That feedback was humbling but invaluable.

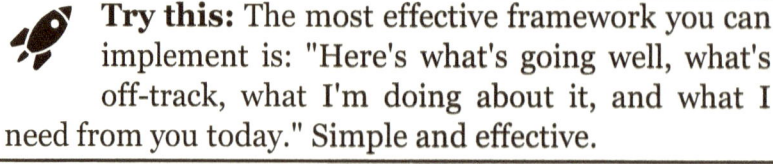 **Try this:** Now I follow what I call the "3-3-3 Rule": If you had 3 minutes, 3 slides, or 3 sentences to pitch your strategy to busy decision-makers, what would you communicate?

Strategic communication means:

- Lead with conclusions, not background
- Focus on impacts, not activities
- Use "executive summaries" to brief leadership quickly
- Adapt your language to match their priorities
- Know when to escalate issues versus handle them independently

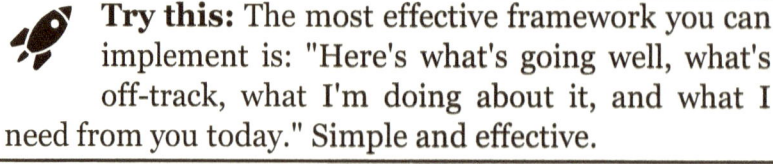 **Try this:** The most effective framework you can implement is: "Here's what's going well, what's off-track, what I'm doing about it, and what I need from you today." Simple and effective.

Your Managing Up Operating System

Just as self-management requires a personal operating system, managing up demands its own systematic approach. This OS determines how you:

- Build relationships with leadership
- Provide updates and share information
- Escalate issues and problems
- Request resources and support
- Navigate organizational changes
- Position your team's work

My managing up OS includes stakeholder mapping, pre-planned communication touchpoints, and a decision framework that clarifies when I handle issues independently versus when I involve my manager.

If you don't develop an intentional system for managing up, you'll default to reactive, inconsistent interactions that undermine your overall effectiveness.

Framework: The Stakeholder Alignment Map

Here's a practical framework I've developed and shared with hundreds of managers:

Stakeholder Alignment Map Template

- **Key Stakeholders:** Direct boss, skip-level managers, cross-functional leaders
- **Their Priorities:** What matters most to each of them?

- **Communication Preferences:** Formal meetings? Data-driven updates? Informal check-ins?
- **Alignment Areas:** Where do you naturally support their goals?
- **Potential Tensions:** Where might your priorities potentially conflict?
- **Influence Strategy:** Your plan to support, inform, and align with each stakeholder

I recommend completing this exercise as priorities and relationships meaningfully evolve. One marketing director I coached used this framework to transform a strained relationship with her CMO, moving from tense weekly interactions to becoming a trusted strategic partner within a matter of months.

Use Case: Managing Up During Organizational Change

During a company-wide reorganization at a Telco firm where I worked, I made it a priority to understand how the changes would affect my boss's role and goals. While other managers focused solely on protecting their teams and territories, I helped my boss prepare for his expanded responsibilities and connected him with key stakeholders he would need to influence.

When the restructuring settled, our department emerged with expanded responsibilities and resources—largely because we positioned ourselves as solutions to the organization's new challenges rather than defenders of the status quo.

The most effective approach during organizational change:

- Seek to understand the business rationale behind changes
- Help your boss adapt to new expectations or stakeholders
- Be a source of stability for your team while showing flexibility upward
- Look for opportunities within the disruption
- Demonstrate your value in the evolving context

Managing Up in Challenging Situations

The real test of managing up comes in difficult scenarios. Here are two common challenges:

The Micromanager

Bob the micromanager bulldozes his way through your inbox.

When facing a boss who checks in constantly and questions every decision, the instinct is often to push back or withdraw. Instead, recognize that micromanagement typically stems from anxiety about uncertainty and surprises.

I once mentored one of my peers to implement a simple system: a morning email outlining priorities and progress, and an end-of-day recap highlighting achievements and upcoming risks. About 10 days in, the interruptions decreased dramatically. By proactively providing structure and information, you can reduce your boss's anxiety and earn greater autonomy.

The Absentee Boss

The opposite challenge—a manager who's rarely available and provides minimal guidance—requires a different approach. When I worked for a senior managing director at my firm who traveled constantly, I secured brief weekly phone check-ins during his commute and created a shared document with "Decisions Needed" that he could review asynchronously.

With absent managers, be exceptionally self-directed, find creative ways to get minimal but regular access, and develop clear decision rights: "If I don't hear from you by Thursday, I'll proceed with option A."

The Ethics of Managing Up

A critical note on integrity: managing up is not about manipulation, politics for personal gain, or blind loyalty. It's about creating productive, ethical relationships that serve your team, your boss, and the organization. If you find yourself compromising your values to please a superior, that's not managing up—it's selling out.

True managing up includes having the courage to deliver difficult news when necessary, to respectfully challenge flawed thinking, and to prioritize organizational success above personal advancement. The most respected managers speak truth to power—diplomatically but directly.

A Final Word; Trusting the Unseen Context

One of the most challenging aspects of managing up is learning to trust decisions from your manager that seem opaque or counterintuitive from your vantage point. Your boss operates with a fundamentally different information set than you do—they have access to confidential strategic discussions, budget constraints you're unaware of, political dynamics across departments, and directives from senior leadership that may not be immediately shareable. They also maintain a broader field of vision that encompasses adjacent teams, parallel initiatives, and organizational priorities that extend well beyond your immediate scope of work. While it's natural to want to understand the "why" behind every decision, effective upward management sometimes requires accepting that you simply cannot see the full chess board. This doesn't mean abandoning critical thinking or becoming a passive executor, but rather recognizing that your manager's seemingly inexplicable choices may be the result of constraints, opportunities, or strategic considerations that exist outside your current line of sight. The key is to ask clarifying questions about execution and impact while respecting the boundaries of what can be shared, and to trust that the broader context—even when invisible to you—is informing the decision-making process.

Key Takeaways

↳ Managing up is a leadership skill, not politics—it's about leading without formal authority

↳ Understanding your manager's world creates the foundation for effective upward influence

↳ Aligning your priorities with organizational goals ensures your work gets support

↳ Strategic communication builds trust: focus on impact and outcomes, not just activities

↳ Develop a system for managing up that works for your specific leadership context

↳ Different challenges require different approaches—adapt your strategy accordingly

↳ Effective managing up creates a multiplier effect that benefits your team and organization

Head over to **https://www.man-ageros.work/chapter2** for additional information and templates.

In the next chapter, we'll turn our attention to managing your direct reports—how to transition from individual contributor to manager and become the kind of boss people genuinely want to work for.

3

Managing Individuals (Becoming the Boss People Want)

The Shift From Contributor to Manager

"You're great at solving problems, but it feels like you don't trust us to solve things ourselves."

When one of my team members shared this feedback, it stopped me in my tracks. I had recently transitioned from being a high-performing individual contributor to a management role—and I was still operating in doer mode: jumping in to fix problems, taking over in critical moments, and focusing on my own output rather than enabling others.

T his insight revealed one of the most challenging transitions in any professional journey. Most new managers are promoted because they excel at the *work*. But as a manager, your value isn't measured by your personal output—it's measured by your team's collective performance. This requires a fundamental shift from *doing the work* to *developing the people who do the work*.

The transition isn't just about changing what you do—it's about transforming how you think about success itself.

Why People Don't Leave Companies, They Leave Managers

There's profound truth in this familiar saying. Gallup research consistently shows that **the primary reason employees quit is poor management**. When people don't feel heard, supported, or developed, they disengage—or exit.

Early in my career, I reported to a manager who only initiated contact when something went wrong. I never received constructive feedback, rarely felt valued, and had no clear vision of what success looked like. Eventually, I began to check out emotionally. That experience left a lasting impression. I promised myself that when I became a manager, I would manage differently. While I made plenty of mistakes along that journey, I learned valuable lessons about what makes people want to stay, grow, and succeed under your management.

> **Try this:** Be a great manager by constantly creating an environment where people feel both challenged and supported—where high performance becomes the natural outcome of strong relationships and clear expectations.

The 5 Disciplines of People Management

There are five fundamental disciplines every manager must master to manage people effectively:

1. Build Trust First

Trust forms the foundation of every effective management relationship. Without it, even your best intentions will be questioned, your feedback rejected, and your guidance ignored. Trust isn't granted with your title—it's earned through consistent action, integrity, and genuine care.

When I inherited a team where the previous manager had broken promises and played favorites, I faced a wall of skepticism. I had to demonstrate trustworthiness in every interaction: showing up prepared for meetings, following through on commitments no matter how small, acknowledging what I didn't know, and being transparent about both successes and setbacks.

Trust accelerator: Make and keep small promises consistently before asking for big commitments. Remember that trust accumulates gradually but can evaporate instantly with a single breach.

Trust isn't just about honesty—it's about reliability, consistency, and psychological safety. When your team trusts you, they'll speak up about problems, take appropriate risks, and bring their authentic selves to work.

2. Communicate With Clarity

Most performance issues stem not from capability but from unclear expectations. Ambiguity creates anxiety and wastes energy. Clear communication about goals, roles, and standards allows people to channel their talents productively.

I once launched a major project without explicitly defining decision rights and escalation paths. The result? Weeks of confusion, duplicate efforts, and unnecessary friction. When we paused to clarify who owned what decisions and how information should flow, productivity immediately improved.

Clarity framework: For every significant assignment or goal, ensure alignment on:

- Specific outcomes (What does success look like?)
- Quality standards (What level of excellence is required?)

- Timeline (When is this needed?)
- Resources (What support is available?)
- Constraints (What boundaries must be respected?)
- Check-in points (How will we track progress?)

The clearer your expectations, the more autonomy you can grant your team—because you've established the guardrails for success.

3. Implement Individual Development Constantly

Great managers don't just manage performance—they deliberately grow talent. This means creating personalized development plans, providing stretch opportunities, and helping people connect daily work to long-term career aspirations.

I make it a practice to understand each team member's professional goals, strengths, and growth areas. During my quarterly planning, I map upcoming projects against these development needs. When a strategic project presentation emerged, I assigned it to a team member who needed visibility and presentation experience—rather than handling it myself or giving it to the most seasoned team member that I could trust.

Development catalyst: Use the 70-20-10 model for growth:

- 70% challenging assignments and on-the-job experience
- 20% developmental relationships and feedback
- 10% formal training or education

Development isn't separate from the work—it happens through the work when you're intentional about matching opportunities to growth needs.

4. Give Feedback That Fuels

Feedback is the mechanism through which growth occurs. When delivered effectively, it accelerates development and builds confidence. When withheld or delivered poorly, it stunts a person's development.

I've learned to make feedback a continuous practice, not an annual event. When a team member led a meeting that lacked clear next steps, I shared specific observations immediately afterward: "I noticed participants seemed unclear about action items. Next time, consider capturing decisions and owners in real-time on screen. This will ensure everyone leaves aligned."

Feedback formula: SBI (Situation, Behavior, Impact)

- **Situation**: The specific context
- **Behavior**: The observable actions (not assumptions about intent)
- **Impact**: The effect of those actions on results, others, or the organization

Constructive feedback should feel like a gift—not a weapon or a surprise.

5. Recognize and Motivate

Recognition isn't just about making people feel good—it's about reinforcing what matters and energizing future performance. Different people are motivated by different forms of recognition, from public acknowledgment to new responsibilities to simple appreciation.

I keep a "recognition inventory" for each team member, noting their preferences and meaningful achievements. For one of my more introverted project managers who disliked public spotlights, I send thoughtful emails or Teams messages acknowledging specific contributions and occasionally share their work (with permission) as examples of excellence in team settings.

Recognition principle: Be specific, timely, and aligned with values. "Thank you for staying late" is nice; "Your persistence in solving [name the specific issue] demonstrated your commitment to excellence and saved a key relationship" is powerful and empowering.

Recognition costs little but pays enormous dividends in engagement and discretionary effort.

6. Avoid Other People's Monkeys

I know I said there were 5 disciplines of people management, but I wanted to give you a bonus technique. One of the additional tools in my arsenal when it comes to managing people comes from a 1999 Harvard Business Review article called "Management Time: Who's Got the Monkey?" by William Oncken, Jr. and Donald L. Wass. I've adapted their approach into my daily behavior, and it's transformed how I manage teams (and ultimately free up my own time).

When I first moved into management, I found myself drowning in a sea of tasks that rightfully belonged to my team members. My calendar was packed, my to-do list was endless, and I became the bottleneck for progress.

That's when I discovered the concept of "monkey management."

I now visualize every problem or task as a "monkey" that can jump from one person's back to another. When a team member comes to my office with an issue and leaves with me promising to "look into it," that monkey has effectively jumped from their back to mine. Suddenly, I'm responsible for the next move while they wait.

Last month, my project manager Jessica came to me frustrated. She was stuck between three stakeholders who couldn't agree on development priorities—one wanted reconciliation features, another wanted streamlined cash processing, and the third insisted on investment management tools first.

In the past, I would have jumped in to resolve this myself, effectively taking ownership of her problem. Instead, I used it as a coaching opportunity.

"What approaches have you considered?" I asked. After some initial surprise, Jessica began thinking through options. Through reflective questioning, we brainstormed several approaches: organizing a joint prioritization workshop, developing a phased delivery approach, creating business cases to compare ROI, or escalating for executive decision.

Crucially, I never took ownership of the solution. Jessica chose to facilitate a prioritization workshop with objective criteria, keeping the responsibility firmly with her.

Two days later, she returned energized. The workshop had resolved the impasse and created stakeholder alignment. She had developed a framework balancing urgent operational needs with strategic objectives, and established an ongoing priority management process.

By resisting the urge to solve her problem, I helped Jessica develop both the solution and the capability to handle similar challenges independently.

Unlike many new managers who unconsciously collect these monkeys throughout the day, I've trained myself to keep them where they belong. When team members approach me with problems, I now use four simple steps:

1. I help them clearly define what needs to happen next
2. I ensure they maintain ownership of their monkeys
3. We establish the appropriate level of supervision
4. We set specific follow-up times to check progress

This approach has dramatically shortened my to-do list compared to other managers at my level. My calendar remains manageable, team members develop greater initiative, and problems get solved more efficiently.

> **Try this:** The beauty of this technique is in its simplicity and effectiveness. Keeping "monkeys" with their rightful owners, you can create a more capable team while freeing yourself to focus on your own work.

Your People Management Operating System

Just as you need personal and upward management systems, effective people management requires its own operating system. This OS determines how you:

- Structure one-on-one meetings
- Calibrate performance expectations
- Deliver and receive feedback
- Allocate development opportunities
- Navigate challenging conversations
- Celebrate wins and learn from setbacks

My people management OS includes weekly one-on-ones with a consistent format, monthly development check-ins, quarterly goal setting, and "listening tours" when taking on new teams.

Without an intentional system for managing people, you'll default to reactive, inconsistent management that undermines trust and performance.

Framework: The Weekly One-on-One

One-on-one meetings are the beating heart of effective management. They build relationships, surface issues early, and create accountability. Here's the structure I've refined over years:

Weekly One-on-One Template

- **Check-In:** How are you doing? (personally, and professionally)
- **Priorities Review:** Progress on key goals and upcoming milestones
- **Obstacle Removal:** Blockers I can help with (watch out for monkeys!)
- **Development Focus:** Progress on growth areas
- **Feedback Exchange:** What's working well? What could be better? (both ways)

- **Resource Needs:** Support or tools needed for success
- **Action Items:** Clear next steps for both parties

I recommend 30-45 minutes, with the team member setting the primary agenda. Make these meetings sacred - rescheduling occasionally is inevitable, but canceling sends a devastating message about priorities.

Use Cases: The Art of Individualized Management

Turning Around a Struggling Performer

One of my team members—let's call her Andrea—began missing deadlines and disengaging in meetings. Instead of jumping to conclusions or issuing warnings, I approached with curiosity. During a candid one-on-one, I learned she felt overwhelmed by competing priorities and had unclear expectations.

Together, we reset with crystal-clear success metrics, broke her workload into weekly milestones, and implemented daily 10-minute check-ins for two weeks. She rebounded quickly and went on to lead a successful initiative. What initially looked like a performance problem was actually a clarity and support issue.

The lesson: When someone struggles, assume a systems problem before a people problem. Ask: "What's getting in your way?" before "Why aren't you performing?"

Growing a Future Manager

Another team member, Dan, consistently exceeded expectations. I could have simply appreciated his contributions and let him continue. Instead, I saw potential for more: "I'd like you to manage our next major project milestone. It's a stretch, but I believe you're ready."

I provided the framework, coaching, and visibility he needed—while giving him space to develop his own management style. He faced challenges and made mistakes, but with support and feedback, he grew rapidly. Within eighteen months, he was promoted to manage his own team.

The lesson: Your top performers need challenges more than comfort. Your job is to see potential before they do— and create safe spaces to develop it.

The Ethics of People Management

A note on power: Management comes with significant influence over others' careers, wellbeing, and daily experience. This power demands responsible stewardship.

Ethical people management means:

- Giving credit generously and taking blame readily
- Addressing performance issues directly and respectfully
- Being willing to have difficult conversations
- Making tough decisions with compassion
- Creating fair opportunities for growth and recognition
- Using your position to break down barriers, not create them

The most respected managers I've known wielded their influence to elevate others, not themselves. This isn't always easy to do but keeping this list in your mind's eye will help you become a better, and fairer manager.

Key Takeaways

↳ Your success is now measured through your team's growth and results

↳ Trust forms the foundation of all effective management relationships

↳ Clear communication eliminates the anxiety and wasted energy of ambiguity

↳ Systematic development turns daily work into growth opportunities

↳ Regular, balanced feedback accelerates performance and builds confidence

↳ Recognition reinforces values and energizes future efforts

↳ Avoiding other people's monkeys helps people develop their own skills

↳ Consistent one-on-ones are the heartbeat of effective people management

Head over to **https://www.manageros.work/chapter3** for additional information and templates. In the next chapter, we'll expand your impact further as we explore how to build and manage high-performing teams— moving from managing individuals to creating cohesive units that achieve more together than they ever could separately.

4

Managing and Leading Teams (From Manager to Multiplier)

"To be an effective team leader, you need patience, strength, insight, tenacity and courage. If that doesn't work, bribe them with doughnuts.

The Hidden Team Leadership Dimension

"So who's actually running this project?" The question from our CEO caught me off guard during our quarterly business review.

"I am," I replied confidently.

"Really? Because I'm seeing seven different people making decisions, and they all seem to be waiting for your approval before moving forward."

That moment was illuminating—and humbling. While I thought I was effectively managing my expanded team, I had become the bottleneck. People waited for my input on decisions they could have made themselves. Projects stalled when I was unavailable. Despite having capable team members, I had failed to create a system where leadership was distributed and multiplied throughout the organization.

That experience taught me a crucial lesson: managing a team isn't just about overseeing multiple individuals—it's about creating an environment where collective performance exceeds the sum of individual contributions. The most effective team leaders don't just manage people—they build systems that amplify capability and enable scaled impact.

Why Team Leadership Matters

Leadership evolves dramatically when you move from managing individuals to leading teams. Your value shifts from personal productivity to your ability to create conditions where others thrive collectively.

I discovered this evolution firsthand when I moved from managing a small project team to directing the entire PMO. Initially, I tried to stay involved in every decision and review all work—maintaining the same hands-on approach that had worked with a much smaller group. But as my scope expanded, this approach quickly became unsustainable.

Great team leadership isn't about control—it's about multiplication. When you lead teams effectively, you:

- Create alignment around shared vision and goals
- Build systems that enable distributed decision-making
- Foster a culture where people support and challenge each other
- Develop other leaders who extend your impact
- Design processes that function even in your absence

The transition from manager to multiplier distinguishes those who plateau in middle management from those who scale to senior leadership.

The 3 Pillars of Team Leadership

There are three fundamental pillars every manager needs to master when leading teams:

1. Build Team Culture Intentionally

Culture isn't what you say—it's what you consistently do and reward. Some leaders treat culture as a nice-to-have, but in reality, it's the operating system that determines how your team functions, especially when you're not present.

When I led a technology department through a difficult turnaround, we were dealing with low morale, missed deadlines, and quality issues. Rather than focusing on metrics and people performance, I invested heavily in reshaping the team's culture. We articulated clear values—transparency, accountability, and proactive problem-solving—and then systematically reinforced these through our actions.

In team meetings, we started sharing challenges openly rather than hiding them. We implemented blameless retrospectives after setbacks. We celebrated examples of accountability and proactive problem-solving. Within three months, team performance improved dramatically—not because we changed personnel, but because we changed the environment.

 Try this: Define your team's cultural code by documenting:

- Three to five core values translated into specific behaviors
- How decisions should be made at different levels
- What behaviors will be recognized and rewarded
- Which legacy practices no longer serve the team's mission

Remember: Culture forms whether you shape it intentionally or not. The choice is whether you'll be deliberate about the culture you create within your teams.

2. Align Through Compelling Vision

The second pillar focuses on creating a clear, shared vision that connects daily work to meaningful outcomes. Without this alignment, teams optimize for individual goals rather than collective impact.

I once inherited a complex international acquisition that spanned six European countries, where each function—legal, finance, HR, IT, operations, sales, marketing, and regulatory—operated independently. Each team had its own priorities, creating constant friction and inefficiency. Legal focused only on compliance, finance on tax structures, and country teams defended their local approaches at the expense of global alignment.

My first action was to establish a unified vision centered on value creation through successful integration, with joint outcomes that required cross-functional collaboration across all geographies.

Initially, this change created resistance—teams were used to optimizing for their specialized domains rather than the overall acquisition success. But within 6 weeks, this unified approach transformed how everyone worked together, resulting in higher synergy and a faster integration timeline. By aligning everyone around concrete business outcomes rather than functional excellence, we turned a fragmented effort into a cohesive international team that preserved local market strengths while capturing the full strategic value of the acquisition.

Vision alignment requires:

- A clear, compelling articulation of "where we're going and why it matters"
- Cascading goals that connect individual work to team and organizational outcomes
- Regular reinforcement that ties daily tasks to bigger purpose
- Shared metrics that require collaboration rather than optimization of silos

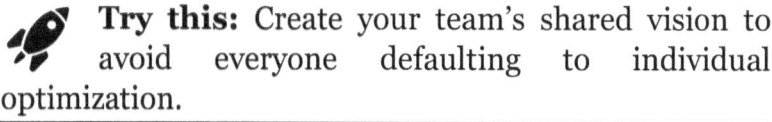 **Try this:** Create your team's shared vision to avoid everyone defaulting to individual optimization.

3. Develop Team Capability Systematically

The third pillar addresses how teams evolve and mature over time. Effective leaders adapt their approach based on the team's developmental stage and deliberately build capability across the group.

As described in Tuckman's influential work on team development (Tuckman, 1965), high-performing teams typically progress through four distinct stages: forming, storming, norming, and performing. Understanding this progression helped me recognize that team conflicts were not failures but often necessary steps toward cohesion.

Tuckman, B. W. (1965). Developmental sequence in small groups. Psychological Bulletin, 63(6), 384-399. https://doi.org/10.1037/h0022100 provides a very useful framework in that I learned that different phases require distinctly different leadership approaches:

Forming Phase: When I built a new cross-functional project team, members were polite but hesitant. During this phase, I provided high clarity on roles, expectations, and objectives. We ran frequent daily standups and spent time on relationship building.

Storming Phase: As the team began working together, conflicts emerged around priorities and working styles. Rather than suppressing this tension, I created structured forums to address differences constructively. This included dedicated retrospectives and working agreements that acknowledged diverse perspectives.

Norming Phase: As productive patterns emerged, we codified successful practices into team routines and celebrated emerging norms. This included documentation of decision processes and communication protocols that had proven effective.

Performing Phase: Once the team reached high performance, I shifted to an outcomes-based leadership approach, maximizing autonomy and minimizing interference. My role became primarily removing obstacles and connecting the team to broader organizational context.

Understanding this developmental cycle prevents common leadership mistakes—like micromanaging a performing team or providing too little structure for a forming team.

Your Team Leadership Operating System

Just as self-management requires a personal operating system and managing up demands its own systematic approach, team leadership requires a deliberate system that determines how you:

- Make and distribute decisions
- Communicate vision and priorities
- Build and reinforce culture
- Develop capability across the team
- Handle conflicts and challenges
- Evaluate collective performance

My team leadership OS includes weekly team rhythm meetings, monthly capability assessments, quarterly vision reinforcement sessions, and a decision rights framework that clarifies who makes which decisions and how.

Without an intentional system for team leadership, you'll default to inconsistent approaches that create confusion and undermine collective performance.

Level Up: Manager to Multiplier

Here's a practical framework you can leverage from Liz Wiseman's groundbreaking book "Multipliers: How the Best Leaders Make Everyone Smarter" which she co-authored with Greg McKeown. Published in 2010, with an expanded edition released in 2017, this work has become influential in leadership development and organizational psychology.

The Multiplier Matrix

Dimension	Diminisher Behaviors	Multiplier Behaviors
Decision-Making	Centralized with leader	Pushed to appropriate level
Information Flow	Controlled and filtered	Open and transparent
Mistakes	Punished or hidden	Treated as learning opportunities
Credit	Claimed by leader	Distributed to contributors
Problem-Solving	Leader provides solutions	Team develops capabilities

I recommend reviewing the above matrix quarterly, honestly assessing where your leadership practices fall on the spectrum. One technology director I coached used this framework to transform her leadership approach, moving from being seen as controlling to becoming known for developing strong, autonomous teams within a year.

Use Case: Scaling Team Performance

When my company acquired a competitor, I was tasked with integrating and leading the combined department—increasing my team from 8 to 25 people overnight. It was clear my previous hands-on approach wouldn't scale.

Instead of trying to maintain control, I implemented a team-of-teams structure with clear domains and decision rights. We created a leadership layer with empowered team leads, implemented cross-team coordination mechanisms, and established shared goals that required collaboration.

Within six months, the integrated team was delivering more effectively than either organization had before the merger.

The most effective approach for scaling team performance:

- Create clear domains with real ownership and accountability
- Develop a lightweight coordination system that prevents silos
- Implement shared metrics that reinforce collaboration
- Build capability in emerging leaders through deliberate coaching
- Design systems that don't depend on your personal involvement

Team Leadership in Challenging Situations

The real test of team leadership comes in difficult scenarios. Here are two common challenges:

The Fragmented Team

When I inherited a team with deep functional divides and trust issues, my instinct was to focus immediately on performance metrics. Instead, I recognized the underlying dynamics needed addressing first.

We implemented a series of structured team experiences designed to build relationships across boundaries—

including paired problem-solving exercises, cross-functional projects, and facilitated discussions about team dynamics. By investing in the team's foundation before pushing for performance outcomes, we ultimately achieved stronger results with greater sustainability.

The Crisis Situation

During a major technical outage that directly impacted our customers, I observed how crisis reveals team culture. Teams with strong foundations pull together; fragmented teams fall apart.

Rather than taking control and issuing directives, I focused on creating conditions for the team to respond effectively: establishing clear roles, ensuring information flowed freely, removing obstacles, and maintaining calm focus on priorities. By trusting the team's capability rather than centralizing control, we resolved the crisis more effectively and emerged stronger.

The Ethics of Team Leadership

A critical note on integrity: team leadership is not about creating dependency or building your personal empire (in fact, smaller teams are better!) It's about developing capability and fostering an environment where people can do their best work in service of meaningful company objectives.

True team leadership includes having the courage to distribute power, develop potential successors, and put the team's success above personal recognition. The most respected team leaders aren't those who create dependence on their presence—they're those who build sustainable systems that thrive even in their absence.

Key Takeaways

⮡ Team leadership requires evolving from controlling to multiplying impact

⮡ Culture isn't optional—it's the operating system that determines how your team performs

⮡ Vision creates alignment only when it connects to daily work and shared metrics

⮡ Teams develop through predictable stages, each requiring different leadership approaches

⮡ Decision rights and information flow determine whether you enable or constrain your team

⮡ Scale comes from building systems, not from working harder or longer

⮡ The true measure of your leadership is what happens when you're not in the room

Head over to **https://www.manageros.work/chapter4** for additional information and templates.

In the next chapter, we'll explore how these team leadership principles apply in remote and distributed environments—where intentional systems and clear communication become even more critical to success.

5

Managing Remote Employees (Leading From Anywhere)

"You're working back at the office now, Bob. The jammies need to go.

The Remote Management Challenge

"I don't understand why we're missing deadlines. Everyone seems busy collaborating on Zoom calls, but projects aren't moving forward." My colleague, a newly remote director of lab operations, was frustrated. His previously high-performing team was struggling with the transition to distributed work.

As we dug deeper, the problem became clear: He was trying to recreate office-based management practices in a virtual environment. Daily stand-ups had become tedious status meetings. He was scheduling constant check-ins to maintain "visibility" into work. Team members felt simultaneously micromanaged and disconnected.

That experience reinforced what I'd learned from years of leading distributed teams: Remote management isn't simply traditional management conducted through a webcam. It's a distinct discipline requiring deliberate design and new rituals.

The most effective remote managers don't try to replicate the office virtually—they build something better by leveraging the unique advantages of distributed work while addressing its inherent challenges.

Why Remote Management Matters

Remote work fundamentally changes how information flows, how trust forms, and how culture develops. Without intentional management, these changes can undermine everything from decision speed to team cohesion.

I discovered this firsthand when I transitioned from managing co-located teams to managing a global organization spanning five different time zones. Initially, I struggled with basic coordination—meetings favored headquarters' working hours, information shared in person never reached remote team members, and distance workers felt like second-class citizens.

Effective remote management isn't just about maintaining productivity—it's about creating environments where distributed teams can thrive. When you manage hybrid or remote teams successfully, you:

- Build trust without the benefit of physical proximity
- Create communication systems that work across time and space
- Ensure equitable participation regardless of location
- Maintain team culture without shared physical space
- Prevent isolation and burnout despite distance

The ability to manage effectively across distance has become an essential skill—separating those who can build high-performing teams regardless of location from those limited by geography.

The 3 Pillars of Remote Management

There are three fundamental pillars every manager needs to master when managing remote teams:

1. Build Trust Without Proximity

Trust forms differently in remote environments. In offices, trust often develops through informal interactions and observation. In distributed teams, it must be constructed more deliberately.

When I managed a project team distributed across three countries, I initially struggled to build cohesion. Team members were competent individually but hesitant to collaborate across locations. I realized that without the foundation of trust, our geographic distribution was becoming an insurmountable barrier.

We implemented several trust-building practices: consistent weekly one-on-ones that started with personal check-ins, transparent documentation of decisions and rationales, and a practice of explicitly recognizing contributions across the distributed team. Most importantly, I became rigorously reliable—keeping commitments, starting meetings on time, and following through on promises.

Within two months, cross-location collaboration increased dramatically. Trust wasn't built through proximity—it was built through intentionality.

Try this: Develop trust-building rituals by:

- Creating consistent meeting rhythms that team members can depend on
- Making your thinking visible by sharing context and reasoning, not just decisions
- Dedicating time for personal connection at the start of team interactions
- Being exceptionally reliable in your commitments to remote team members

Remember: Remote teams don't trust managers because they see them often; they trust managers who communicate with intention and follow through consistently.

2. Design Communication Architecture

The second pillar addresses how information flows in distributed environments. Without hallway conversations and impromptu discussions, communication must be deliberately architected.

When my financial services firm shifted to a hybrid model, miscommunication became our biggest challenge. Information shared in office conversations never reached remote colleagues. Remote workers felt perpetually out of the loop, while in-office staff grew frustrated by having to document everything.

Rather than trying to replicate office communication, we designed a new system from scratch. We established clear channels for different types of communication— asynchronous updates in shared documents, decision discussions in dedicated chat channels, and synchronous collaboration in focused video meetings. Most importantly, we established norms around which channels were appropriate for different types of information.

 Try this: Build your remote communication ruleset:

- **Asynchronous by default**: Using documentation, recorded videos, and shared updates as the primary information flow
- **Synchronous by exception**: Reserving real-time meetings for collaboration, relationship-building, and complex problem-solving
- **Clear channel purpose**: Defining exactly which tools are used for what type of communication
- **Time zone equity**: Rotating meeting times to share the burden of early or late calls across the team

A team I advised struggled with endless video meetings until they implemented a simple rule: "If it can be an email or document, it shouldn't be a meeting." Meeting time decreased drastically while information sharing actually improved. Collaboration tools like Teams and Slack make it even easier nowadays to succeed with remotely distributed teams.

3. Cultivate Culture Across Distance

The third pillar focuses on maintaining cohesion and shared identity despite physical separation. Culture in remote teams isn't accidental—it must be deliberately developed.

After acquiring a European company, our U.S.-headquartered organization struggled to integrate the remote team into our culture. Despite shared goals and complementary skills, there was a persistent "us vs. them" dynamic that undermined collaboration.

We tackled this by explicitly codifying our shared values and creating virtual rituals that reinforced them. We implemented a "weekly wins" practice where team members recognized colleagues who exemplified our values. We created cross-location projects with shared outcomes. Most significantly, we invested in periodic in-person gatherings that built relationships that sustained remote collaboration for months afterward.

 Try this: Build your remote culture rules:

- **Explicit values documentation**: Clearly articulating what your team stands for
- **Shared rituals**: Creating regular practices that reinforce connection and identity
- **Recognition systems**: Establishing ways for team members to celebrate contributions
- **Periodic in-person connection**: When possible, bringing people together to strengthen bonds

A technology manager I coached implemented virtual "coffee roulette" pairings that randomly connected team members across locations for informal conversations. This simple practice dramatically increased cross-functional collaboration and reduced the sense of isolation.

Your Remote Management Operating System

Just as previous management domains require systematic approaches, remote management demands an intentional operating system that determines how you:

- Coordinate across time zones and geographies
- Create visibility into work without surveillance
- Build and maintain relationships at a distance
- Prevent isolation and burnout despite separation
- Develop culture without shared physical space

My remote management OS includes asynchronous communication, dedicated relationship-building rituals, workload monitoring systems, and clear documentation requirements—all designed to overcome the inherent challenges of distance.

Without an intentional system for remote management, you'll default to either excessive control or dangerous neglect—both paths lead to disengagement and underperformance.

Framework: The Remote Clarity Map

Here's a practical framework I've been using with remote teams:

The Remote Clarity Map

Domain	Questions to Answer	Documentation Approach
Goals & Priorities	What outcomes matter most? How do individual priorities connect to team objectives?	Shared objectives document with weekly updates
Availability & Access	When are team members working? How quickly should people respond to	Team calendar with working hours and response expectations

	different communication types?	
Decision Rights	Who can decide what? What requires consultation vs. approval?	Decision matrix specifying authority levels
Communication Channels	Which tools for what purpose? When to use synchronous vs. asynchronous methods?	Channel guide with specific use cases for Teams, Email, and Confluence
Progress Visibility	How will work status be shared? How are blockers raised?	Regular status update format and schedule

I recommend reviewing this map quarterly and sharing it with all team members. One engineering director implemented this approach when her previously co-located team went remote during the pandemic, reducing confusion and increasing decision speed significantly.

Managing Through Time Zone Challenges

When I managed a global technology team spanning Asia, Europe, and North America, time zones posed our greatest challenge. Initially, team members in Asia felt marginalized because most meetings occurred during U.S. business hours.

Instead of accepting this inequity, we implemented a comprehensive solution:

- Established core collaboration hours (3-4 hours where at least 2 regions had core overlap with each other)
- Created a rotating schedule for meetings that shared the burden of early/late calls
- Developed robust asynchronous documentation practices so decisions didn't require everyone to be online simultaneously
- Paired team members across regions with complementary skills and shared responsibilities

Within one quarter, our cross-region collaboration improved dramatically, and team members in all locations reported feeling equally valued and included.

 Try this: Implement these practices for your remote team:

- Design for asynchronous progress as the default
- Rotate the inconvenience of off-hours meetings fairly
- Document decisions and context thoroughly
- Create social connections that span geographic boundaries

Remote Management in Challenging Situations

The real test of remote management comes in difficult scenarios. Here are two common challenges:

The Disengaged Remote Team Member

When a previously high-performing business analyst became increasingly withdrawn in our remote environment—missing deadlines and participating minimally in meetings—my instinct was to increase check-ins and monitoring. Instead, I scheduled an open-ended conversation focused on understanding their experience.

I discovered they were struggling with isolation and unclear expectations. We developed a solution together: connecting them with a peer "collaboration partner" for regular interaction, creating clearer deliverable specifications, and establishing a more structured check-in rhythm. Within three weeks, both engagement and performance improved dramatically.

The key insight: Remote disengagement often stems from isolation or uncertainty, not lack of commitment. Address the root causes rather than adding surveillance.

The Hybrid Team Divide

After our partial office reopening post Covid created a hybrid environment, an unhealthy dynamic emerged between in-office and remote employees. Information asymmetry developed, with in-office employees having access to spontaneous conversations and decision contexts that remote employees missed.

Rather than accepting this two-tier system, we implemented several interventions:

- "Digital first" communication for all important information, regardless of where people were located
- Meeting equity practices (either everyone on video or everyone in person)
- Rotation of meeting times to prevent headquarters dominance
- Regular virtual social events that remote employees could fully participate in

By refusing to accept the natural drift toward office-centricity, we maintained an inclusive culture where location didn't determine influence or access.

The Ethics of Remote Management

A critical note on integrity: remote management creates unique ethical considerations around surveillance, boundaries, and equity. The temptation to implement monitoring software or expect always-on availability can be strong when you can't physically see your team.

True remote management respects privacy and autonomy while creating appropriate visibility into work outcomes. It recognizes that remote work blurs the boundary between professional and personal life—and takes responsibility for helping team members maintain healthy separation.

The most respected remote managers don't treat distance as a deficit to be overcome through control—they see it as an opportunity to build systems based on trust, clarity, and shared purpose.

Key Takeaways

↳ Remote management isn't watered-down management—it's a specialized discipline requiring deliberate design

↳ Trust in distributed teams is built through consistency, transparency, and intentional connection

↳ Communication architecture should optimize for clarity and inclusion, not convenience

↳ Performance visibility comes from well-designed systems, not surveillance

↳ Culture transcends physical space when built on shared values, rituals, and recognition

↳ Time zone equity requires intentional rotation and asynchronous processes

↳ The greatest remote management test is building genuine human connection across digital space

Head over to **https://www.manageros.work/chapter5** for additional information and templates.

Whether managing a fully distributed team or navigating the complexities of hybrid arrangements, these principles will help you create environments where people can do their best work—regardless of where that work happens.

Conclusion: Your ManagerOS - The Continuous Upgrade

"IMPLEMENTING THESE CHANGES WON'T BE EASY. WE'RE PRETTY SET IN DOING THINGS THE WRONG WAY.

"So what's next for you?" The question came from a senior executive who had watched me develop from a struggling first-time manager to a management coach over the span of fifteen years.

I paused, reflecting on my journey. "Honestly, I'm still figuring that out," I admitted. "But I know whatever comes next will build on what I've learned about management—that it's never finished, only continuously improved."

She smiled knowingly. "That's exactly why you've been successful. Most managers install an approach and never update it again."

This conversation crystallized the most important lesson from my decades in management: the most effective managers treat their approach as an operating system requiring regular updates and improvements. They never mistake experience for expertise or comfort for mastery.

Integrating Your Management Domains

Throughout this book, we've explored distinct dimensions of management:

- **Self-Management**: Your foundation for personal effectiveness
- **Managing Up**: Tools for leading without authority, as we explored in Chapter 2
- **Managing Direct Reports**: Systems for supervising individuals with clarity and care

- **Team Management**: Frameworks for multiplying rather than controlling
- **Remote Management**: Approaches for bridging digital distance

The greatest challenge isn't mastering these domains individually—it's integrating them into a cohesive approach that adapts to changing circumstances. You might excel at managing up but struggle with remote management or effectively manage individuals while failing to scale your impact through teams.

Great management requires both depth in each domain and the ability to move fluidly between them as situations demand. Consider these integration scenarios:

- When a reorganization puts you under a new boss (managing up) while simultaneously requiring you to rebuild team culture (team management)
- When a direct report is struggling with remote work challenges (remote management) that require you to adjust your coaching approach (managing direct reports)
- When increased responsibilities demand better personal prioritization (self-management) while also requiring you to influence senior leaders with limited face time (managing up)

Integration isn't about perfection in every domain. It's about recognizing which management and leadership skills each situation demands and deliberately applying the right tools from your expanded toolkit.

Your Management Development Cycle

Jim Collins introduced the concept of the "flywheel"—the idea that success comes not from dramatic transformations but from consistently pushing in the right direction until momentum builds. Your management development follows this same principle.

The **ManagerOS** improvement cycle looks like this:

1. **Self-awareness** → Understanding your strengths, gaps, and impact
2. **Deliberate practice** → Applying new approaches in real situations
3. **Feedback collection** → Seeking input on your effectiveness
4. **Reflection and adjustment** → Learning and refining your approach
5. Return to increased self-awareness

Each rotation builds momentum. The manager who completes this cycle consistently—even imperfectly—will outpace those who seek shortcuts or remain comfortable with their current capabilities.

A software development manager I coached initially resisted feedback about his directive style. But by committing to this cycle—practicing more collaborative approaches, actively seeking input from his team, and reflecting honestly on outcomes—he transformed both his effectiveness and his team's performance within six months.

The Three Levels of Management Mastery

As you continue your management journey, recognize that mastery evolves through three distinct levels:

Level 1: Technical Management

Initially, your focus is on mastering the mechanics of management—running effective meetings, delivering feedback, setting goals, and managing performance. This technical foundation is essential but insufficient.

Level 2: Psychological Management

As you develop, you recognize that management is fundamentally psychological—understanding motivations, building trust, navigating resistance to change, and creating environments where people can do their best work.

Level 3: Systemic Management

The highest level involves seeing and influencing entire systems—understanding how culture, processes, incentives, and structures interact to enable or constrain performance across teams and organizations.

Your goal isn't simply to progress through these levels but to develop fluency in all three—addressing technical, psychological, and systemic dimensions of management as situations require.

Managing Through Uncertainty

If there's one certainty in modern management, it's uncertainty itself. The pandemic forced overnight transitions to remote work. AI is transforming knowledge work. Economic conditions shift rapidly. Organizational priorities evolve with increasing frequency.

The most valuable management skill isn't mastering today's challenges—it's developing the adaptability to navigate tomorrow's unknown landscape.

This requires:

- **Continuous learning** – Actively seeking new perspectives and approaches
- **Comfort with discomfort** – Willingly stepping into unfamiliar territory
- **Intellectual humility** – Recognizing the limitations of your current knowledge
- **Decisive experimentation** – Testing new approaches with appropriate speed and rigor

One technology manager I worked with faced a massive cloud migration during a period of rapid growth. Rather than pretending to have all the answers, he established "learning loops"—rapid experiments with clear success criteria and deliberate reflection. This approach turned uncertainty from a threat into a source of competitive advantage.

The Management Legacy Question

"What will remain after you're gone?"

This question has shaped my approach to management more than any other. It shifts focus from immediate results to lasting impact—from what you accomplish to what you enable others to accomplish in your absence.

The most meaningful aspects of my management career aren't visible on a resume—they're found in the managers I've developed, the teams I've built that continue to thrive, and the work processes I've helped shape that outlasted my tenure.

Your management legacy isn't defined by your highest title or biggest achievement. It's defined by:

- The people who grew under your guidance
- The teams that functioned better because of your approach
- The organization that operates more effectively due to your influence
- The problems that remain solved after you've moved on

Consider regularly: "If I left tomorrow, what would continue and what would collapse?" This question reveals both your greatest contributions and your most important work ahead.

Your Next Management Upgrade

As we conclude, I want to offer specific next steps for continuing your management development:

1. **Conduct a comprehensive self-audit** using the frameworks from each chapter. Where are you strongest? Where do you need development?
2. **Seek structured feedback** from those you lead, peers, and your own manager about your effectiveness across each domain.
3. **Identify your highest-leverage growth area** – the management dimension that, if improved,

would most significantly enhance your overall effectiveness.

4. **Create deliberate practice opportunities** – situations where you can apply new approaches in low-risk environments before facing high-stakes challenges.

5. **Build your management learning network** – connect with other developing managers to share insights, challenges, and approaches.

Remember that management growth isn't linear—it's cyclical and sometimes messy. You'll master certain skills only to face new challenges that reveal fresh development needs. This isn't failure; it's the natural progression of management.

Final Thoughts

Management is ultimately an act of service—to your team members, your organization, and your broader purpose. The best managers don't seek control for its own sake but for the positive impact they can create through others.

As you continue refining your **ManagerOS**, remember that technical excellence matters, but human connection endures. As we saw in Chapter 2 on managing up, understanding the human element—the needs, priorities, and preferences of those we work with—is essential for effective management at all levels.

In the words of Theodore Roosevelt: "People don't care how much you know until they know how much you care." This wisdom cuts to the heart of truly effective management. Going through the motions—holding the required meetings, delivering feedback, and making decisions—will never be enough. Your team members can sense when your actions are merely performative versus when they stem from genuine concern for their growth and wellbeing. The most influential managers are those who authentically invest in their people, who see beyond productivity metrics to the whole person, and who demonstrate through consistent actions that their care is real.

Your management journey isn't ending—it's evolving. The skills you've developed provide a foundation for continuous growth, greater impact, and more meaningful contributions. But remember that these skills must be animated by genuine care to truly transform lives and organizations.

I'm grateful you've allowed me to accompany you on this journey so far. Now, the next step is yours to design and implement. Manage and lead with both competence and compassion, with both strategy and sincerity.

Your management and leadership legacy begins today— not just through what you do, but through how authentically you care while doing it.

Additional Resources

Visit **https://www.managerOS.work** to access:

↳ Downloadable frameworks from each chapter

↳ Self-assessment tools to evaluate your current capabilities

↳ Implementation guides for key management practices

Continue your growth journey with support, structure, and proven approaches. Your teams deserve your best management—and so do you.

About the Author

Peter Badger has spent 35 years managing teams across startups, mid-sized enterprises, and at global corporations. With deep roots in technology, finance, and operations, Peter's management journey spans Wall Street, Silicon Valley, and many international boundaries.

From systems analyst to founder, from team lead to executive, he's lived every rung of the management ladder—and knows the difference between simply managing and actually leading teams.

Now, Peter brings his hard-earned lessons to a new generation of professionals. As the creator of **ManagerOS™**, he helps rising managers navigate the messy realities of corporate life with clarity, confidence, and credibility.

www.ingramcontent.com/pod-product-compliance
Lightning Source LLC
Chambersburg PA
CBHW031244120626
46545CB00007B/2634